WORD MADE FLESH

WORD
made
FLESH

Meditations of the Saints
on the Sacred Heart

STEFAN UDELL

Angelico Press

Book and cover design
by Michael Schrauzer

CONTENTS

INTRODUCTION

The Sacred Heart of Jesus begins with the Immaculate Heart of Mary. He received his Heart of flesh from her, and he was for a time sustained by the beating of her heart. Through her heart, she loved her son more than all human hearts, and so loved God in a way and degree that no one else has. She knows the way into the depths of her son's Heart because it is the sole object of her own heart, without exception. Therefore, at the start of each section of this book there is a meditation on our Lady's heart, as a guide for how to approach her son's Heart. Each section is a collection of meditations[1] on an aspect of Christ's Heart, culminating in the penultimate section, on the piercing of the Heart. The Sacred Heart is the instrument of our salvation, and Mary wants to show us this.

Many saints say that meditation on the Passion is the most efficacious mode of prayer, through which we can receive all God desires to give us in prayer. At the conclusion of the Passion, the Sacred Heart was pierced and became a fountain out of which flowed the water and the blood, and from which the Church was born. In prayer, hearts can enter this pierce, and dive into this gently singing, eternally life-giving fountain, like a counterpoint melody harmonizing with the symphony of God's love. Christ first sings into hearts this sweet symphony of love, calling all to himself from the moment of conception. If the doors of hearts open, ears open to the symphony, eyes open to the light, and sweet fragrance is inhaled.

An instrument proceeds from the Sacred Heart to all hearts. Christ plays a song on it to the Father, perfecting praise in devout hearts. Our sin muffles this melody, often to silence. The love of Christ's Heart is the only power that can detach us from sin and strong affections for worldly things. The Word is a two-edged sword, sharp to cut off these affections. This is one great paradox of the Sacred Heart, that it is a weapon and also contains the pierce of a weapon. When Peter cut off the soldier's ear at Gethsemane, Christ restrained him. He was bringing a more powerful

---

[1] While the preponderance of meditations are from the saints, we have also included a select few from Scripture as well as from notable popes, mystics, and theologians.

sword, to cut off from us the eternal consequences of our sin and so to enable us to unite our hearts with his in a symphony of love.

After the Passion, Christ rebuilt the temple, He rose from the grave. In the center of all souls is a place for this temple. It is the abode of an un-divided Love, one from and for God alone. When we receive the Eucharist we receive his resurrected Heart as our temple, and an exchange of hearts occurs. When Jesus places a heart into his own, it is purified in this burning furnace of love, so that we can always remain in this temple, in the light of his life. It is an abode in which no affection, no sin interferes with God's love. Hearts come to cherish this burn, because they are being purified like gold, in light of what Christ has promised. In response we can say, "Be Thou the heart of my heart, the soul of my soul, the spirit of my spirit, the life of my life, and the sole principle of all my thoughts, words, and actions, the faculties of my soul and of all my senses, both interior and exterior."

Like an instrument, our exterior senses can be tuned to our interior senses. We remember our interior spiritual senses so that our physical senses can be converted to the spiritual reality wherein the Love is shared between the Father and the Son. All affections, all senses, all experiences are centered in hearts. It is the command center. All persons have a heart because God has a Heart. All hearts are but an image of his Heart. His Heart is the source of all hearts and so all true hearts are found in him. His Heart was also the command center for his senses in the Incarnation. Christ experienced what all experience, but without sin. His Heart's response to his Creation, to all lights, sounds, smells, tastes, textures, is the model of love for our hearts. He knew that "in everything God works for good with those who love him." His Heart is like an instrument, the oboe that God the Concertmaster wants us to tune our lives to. He gives all who ask his eyes, his ears, his mouth, his hands, his feet, his Heart. His Love, the Holy Spirit, guides hearts to conform to his.

God in his mercy works in hearts despite their sinfulness and weakness. If they turn to God, he sings his love song into them, one that harmonizes apparent contradictions, makes a sweet melody out of suffering, sets the rhythm of heartbeats firm. If only he is asked, if only hearts submit to him with the trust of a child. This book is meant to aid in the turning of hearts to God. There is a symphony in the words of the saints, one that our hearts can join. Mary, through your Immaculate Heart, pray for us.

If your mind eagerly pants to behold these things, keep quiet. Do not strive except against being accustomed to material things. Conquer that habit and you are victorious over all. . . . We seek unity, the simplest thing of all. Therefore let us seek it in simplicity of heart. "Be still and know that I am God." This is not the stillness of idleness but of thought, free from space and time. Swelling fleeting phantasms do not permit us to see abiding unity.

OPENING

EPHESIANS 3:17–19

And that Christ may dwell in your hearts through faith;
that you, being rooted and grounded in love, may
have power to comprehend with all the saints what is
the breadth and length and height and depth, and to
know the love of Christ which surpasses knowledge,
that you may be filled with all the fulness of God.

WISDOM 11:20

But you have arranged all things
by measure and number and weight.

COLOSSIANS 3:14–15

And over all these things put on love, which binds everything
together in perfect harmony. And let the peace of Christ rule in
your hearts, to which indeed you were called in the one body.

1. ST. BERNARD OF CLAIRVAUX

Open, Blessed Virgin
your heart to confidence
your lips to consent, your
womb to its Creator

See, the desire of all
nations knocks at its door
the angel awaits you
he must return to God

If he should pass along
while you are delaying
you would begin again
with sorrow to seek Him

Arise, hasten, open
arise by faith in Him
hasten by devotion
open by your consent

Behold, she said to him,
the handmaid of the Lord
be it done unto me
according to thy word

2. ST. FRANCIS DE SALES

The Spirit smites sinners' hearts
and rouses us to come forth,
out from our iniquity.

Does not such rousing, kindling
of the soul to better things
come from God? So we are roused.

But we did not rouse ourselves;
the Spirit of God roused us,
and to this end it moved us.

I sleep, but my Heart waketh.
So He calls me by His Love,
I know that it is His voice.

God calls us on a sudden,
and as it were startles us,
in these first workings of grace.

We only feel the movement
which God rouses in our hearts,
and with no action of ours.

3. ST. MARGARET MARY ALACOQUE

The Heart of Jesus is an
inexhaustible fountain
out of which three streams flow.

First is the stream of mercy
which flows down upon sinners
and brings the spirit of
sorrow and repentance.

The second is charity
which brings relief to all those
who are suffering some need,
and especially those
striving for perfection.

They will find from this stream the
help of the holy angels,
means of overcoming
all their difficulties.

The third is of love and light,
for perfect friends whom He wills
to unite with Himself.

To these He communicates
His knowledge and way of life
in order that they may give
themselves up completely to
furthering His glory,
each one in his own way.

4. ST. BERNARD OF CLAIRVAUX

It is the Spirit

Nothing is as pleasant to hear
or read with as much interest
as frequently in remembrance
or as sweet upon reflection
as the humanity of Christ
the things He did or commanded
while He was on earth, in the flesh

Notice that the love of the heart

is, in a certain sense, carnal
Souls at prayer should have before them
a Sacred image, the God-man
This image must bind the soul with
the love of virtue and expel
carnal vices, eliminate
temptations and quiet desires

the flesh

who gives life

The measure of such love is this
Its sweetness seizes the whole heart
draws it completely from the love
of flesh and sensual pleasure
This is to love with the whole heart
To love with the whole heart is to
love His Sacred humanity

above everything that tempts us

from within us or without us
A great gift is this devotion
to the humanity of Christ
a gift of the Holy Spirit
This carnal love is worthwhile, since
sensual love is excluded
the world is condemned and conquered

profits nothing.

5. ST. MARGARET MARY ALACOQUE

In the things of God
one must be content
to follow His lead.
Let grace do its work;
follow with all your strength.

The devotion to
the Heart of Jesus
must never be forced.
He wants to whisper
Himself into hearts

softly and sweetly,
through kind charity,
like a precious balm,
perfume, and unction,
spreading gently through.

Let us not worry
if we do not see
our desires for the
glory of this Heart
accomplished at once.

He permits delay
only because of
the pleasure He takes
in seeing our will,
our desire for growth.

6. HANS URS VON BALTHASAR

And the Word came into the world,
Eternal Life chose for itself
the abode of a human Heart.
It deigned to let itself be struck.
His death was a settled affair.
The source of life is defenseless.

In His eternal citadel
God had been unassailable,
a fortress of eternal rest.
The arrows of sin ricocheted
from His most brazen majesty
as if they were children's play-darts.

But God housed in a human Heart!
How easy He was now to reach!
Much more easily than a man.
For man is not only a heart
but bones and tough muscle-fiber
and cartilage and hardened skin.

But what a target a heart is!
How exposed God had made Himself!
Betrayed the weak spot of His love,
a hailstorm will fall upon Him.
Because love always runs over,
His Heart will also run over.

7. ST. BERNARDINE OF SIENA

Mary's Immaculate Heart

> From this furnace of ardor,
> the Virgin brought forth good works,
> works of the most ardent love.
> From a vase of the best wine
> only the best wine can pour,
> from a very hot furnace
> nothing can come forth not hot,
>
> so from the Mother of Christ
> there could come no word but of   was full of
> the highest love and ardor.
> The words of a wise mistress
> are few but substantial and
> full of meaning, so it is
> approximately seven
>
> times, seven words were said by
> the Blessed Mother of Christ;
> a mystic way to show she

To the angel she spoke twice
and twice to Elizabeth.
She spoke twice to her Son, in

the temple and the marriage;
once to servers at that feast.
At these times she spoke little,
though she spoke at length in praise
of God and in thanksgiving,
sevenfold grace.   *My soul magnifies the Lord*;
here she spoke with God, not men.

These seven words were spoken
in a wonderful degree
and a wonderful order
according to the seven
progressions and acts of love
and they are like seven flames
from the furnace of her heart.

I will put my law within them, and I will write it upon their
hearts; and I will be their God, and they shall be my people...

Thus says the Lord,
who gives the sun for light by day
and the fixed order of the moon and the stars for light by night,
who stirs up the sea so that its waves roar —
the Lord of hosts is His name:
"If this fixed order departs
from before me, says the Lord,
then shall the descendants of Israel cease
from being a nation before me for ever."

Thus says the Lord:
"If the heavens above can be measured,
and the foundations of the earth below can be explored,
then I will cast off all the descendants of Israel
for all that they have done,
says the Lord."

THE BREASTPIECE OF AARON

EXODUS 28:15–30

And you shall make a breastpiece of judgment, in skilled work; like the work of the ephod you shall make it; of gold, blue and purple and scarlet stuff, and fine twined linen shall you make it. It shall be square and double, a span its length and a span its breadth. And you shall set in it four rows of stones. A row of sardius, topaz, and carbuncle shall be the first row; and the second row an emerald, a sapphire, and a diamond; and the third row a jacinth, an agate, and an amethyst; and the fourth row a beryl, an onyx, and a jasper; they shall be set in gold filigree. There shall be twelve stones with their names according to the names of the sons of Israel; they shall be like signets, each engraved with its name, for the twelve tribes. And you shall make for the breastpiece twisted chains like cords, of pure gold; and you shall make for the breastpiece two rings of gold, and put the two rings on the two edges of the breastpiece. And you shall put the two cords of gold in the two rings at the edges of the breastpiece; the two ends of the two cords you shall attach to the two settings of filigree, and so attach it in front to the shoulder-pieces of the ephod. And you shall make two rings of gold, and put them at the two ends of the breastpiece, on its inside edge next to the ephod. And you shall make two rings of gold, and attach them in front to the lower part of the two shoulder-pieces of the ephod, at its joining above the skillfully woven band of the ephod. And they shall bind the breastpiece by its rings to the rings of the ephod with a lace of blue, that it may lie upon the skillfully woven band of the ephod, and that the breastpiece shall not come loose from the ephod. So Aaron shall bear the names of the sons of Israel in the breastpiece of judgment upon his heart, when he goes into the holy place, to bring them to continual remembrance before the Lord. And in the breastpiece of judgment you shall put the Urim and the Thummim, and they shall be upon Aaron's heart, when he goes in before the Lord; thus Aaron shall bear the judgment of the people of Israel upon his heart before the Lord continually.

8

The Virgin wore a yellow robe.
It was patterned with red roses.
Inside these were golden roses,
wonderfully interwoven.
The yellow was humility,
in which she subjected herself
completely to every creature,
the roses, her constant patience
and gentleness in everything,
and the golden roses, her love,
for she did all her works in the
Love of God. Her mantle was green,
woven with bright golden roses,
showing that she always flourished
in good works and holy virtues.
But her tunic was the purest,
shining gold, signifying love.
And just as the tunic is the
garment closest to the body
so love is closest to the heart.

9. ST. JOHN EUDES

Christ teaches that His members
dwell in Him and He in them,
that He is the true Aaron,
and He bears His people's name
engraved in precious jewels
upon His breast, and carries
them in the depths of His Heart.
He is a Father to whom
all His children are dearer
than the apple of His eye.
His endless charity for souls
is pictured in countless ways,
such as in the beloved
disciple resting against
His Heart at the Last Supper
and the repose of the blessed
safe in Abraham's bosom.
He takes His lambs in His arms,
holding them close to His Heart
out of His abundant love.

The sweet Heart of Jesus Christ
in the form of a bright lamp
as luminous as crystal
and burning like a flame.

Overflowing on all sides
with an abundant sweetness,
it distills drops like honey
into all devoted hearts.

The fire, heat of Divine Love,
in which Christ offered Himself
to the Father for us all
on the altar of the cross.

The overflowing sweetness
the superabundance of
the goodness and happiness
He gave, the gift of His Heart.

In that gift we have all things
that are wholesome and needful,
in praise and thanksgiving,
in prayer, love, and desire.

11. ST. MARGARET MARY ALACOQUE

I saw this Divine Heart
as on a throne of flames
more brilliant than the sun,
transparent as crystal.

It had the lance's wound
and a crown of sharp thorns
which signified the pricks
our sins had caused Him.

It was surmounted by
a cross, which signified
that, from the first moment
this Sacred Heart was formed,

the cross was planted there,
and that it was filled full
with all bitternesses
and humiliations.

His Sacred Humanity
would have to suffer through
the whole course of His life
and during His Passion.

He made the breastpiece, in skilled work, like the work of the ephod, of gold, blue and purple and scarlet stuff, and fine twined linen. It was square; the breastpiece was made double, a span its length and a span its breadth when doubled. And they set in it four rows of stones. A row of sardius, topaz, and carbuncle was the first row; and the second row, an emerald, a sapphire, and a diamond; and the third row, a jacinth, an agate, and an amethyst; and the fourth row, a beryl, an onyx, and a jasper; they were enclosed in settings of gold filigree. There were twelve stones with their names according to the names of the sons of Israel; they were like signets, each engraved with its name, for the twelve tribes. And they made on the breastpiece twisted chains like cords, of pure gold; and they made two settings of gold filigree and two gold rings, and put the two rings on the two edges of the breastpiece; and they put the two cords of gold in the two rings at the edges of the breastpiece. Two ends of the two cords they had attached to the two settings of filigree; thus they attached it in front to the shoulder-pieces of the ephod. Then they made two rings of gold, and put them at the two ends of the breastpiece, on its inside edge next to the ephod. And they made two rings of gold, and attached them in front to the lower part of the two shoulder-pieces of the ephod, at its joining above the skillfully woven band of the ephod. And they bound the breastpiece by its rings to the rings of the ephod with a lace of blue, so that it should lie upon the skillfully woven band of the ephod, and that the breastpiece should not come loose from the ephod; as the Lord had commanded Moses.

12. ST. BONAVENTURE

and may my heart ever hunger
with perseverance to the end;   after Thee and feed upon Thee
love, delight, ease and affection,   and may my inmost soul be filled
with humility, discretion,   with the sweetness of Thy Savor;
the praise and glory of Thy name,   and may it ever thirst for Thee,
speak of Thee, and do all things for   fountain of love, fountain of life,
come to Thee, meditate on Thee,   fountain of wisdom and knowledge,
seek for Thee, find Thee, run to Thee,   fountain of the eternal light,
and may it ever compass Thee,   the swelling torrent of pleasure,
the fulness of the house of God;

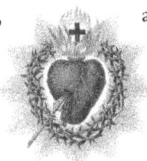

Let My Heart be your temple.
For the rest of My Body
arrange a monastery.
My Sacred Humanity
should henceforth be your cloister.

I know not how to choose well.
There's such sweetness in Your Heart,
In any place out of it
I have no rest or repose,
two things needed in cloisters.

Have you not heard that there are
some who never leave My house
even for food or for rest?
So, choose the places in your
spiritual monastery.

Obeying His sweet commands:
His Hands become my work-room,
His Mouth my reception room,
His Eyes my school, there to read,
His Ears my confessional.

I.ii
THE OCEAN

JOB 28:12–14

But where shall wisdom be found?
And where is the place of understanding?
Man does not know the way to it,
and it is not found in the land of the living.
The deep says, "It is not in me,"
and the sea says, "It is not with me."

ISAIAH 11:9

For the earth shall be full of the knowledge of the Lord
as the waters cover the sea.

14. ST. BERNARD OF CLAIRVAUX

Mary, Star of the Sea;
she is that beautiful
and admirable star,
raised of necessity
above this sea of life,
shining with all virtues.

Turn not thine eyes away
from this star, shining bright,
if thou wouldst not become
engulfed in the tempest.
Winds of temptation rise;
if driven upon the
rocks of tribulation,
look to the shining star,
turn your heart to Mary.

15. ST. JOHN EUDES

Mary, sea of love,
please behold my heart,
the smallest of hearts,
a drop of water,
seeking to unite
with thy vast ocean,
to become lost in
thy depths forever!

Mary, Queen of Hearts,
consecrated to
Jesus, look down on
this tiniest drop,
offered up to thee
to become merged in
the sea of thy love.

16. ST. JOHN EUDES

She sensed in that loving Heart
an endless, shoreless ocean
of love for God His Father,

a possession and an enjoyment
of His singular Divine Goodness,
a repose in His infinite bliss,

a peace passing all understanding,
an incomprehensible treasure
of all the virtues in completeness,

which shone forth in a beauty,
a nobleness, an expanse
and a bright splendor so great

and inexplicable that
there was enough to fill an
infinite number of worlds.

17. ST. MECHTHILD OF HACKEBORN

I am in you and you are in Me,
you live within my omnipotence,
like a fish swimming in the ocean.

What if I get dragged out in a net?

You cannot be drawn away from Me.
Rather, you will make yourself a nest
in the safe place of My Sacred Heart.

How will I know what my nest will be?

Humility in my gifts and grace.
Always plunge yourself deep down into
the abyss of true humility.

Fish are fruitful. What will my fruit be?

When you offer Me to the Father
in joy and glory for all the saints,
then their joys and merits will increase.

18. ST. MARGARET MARY ALACOQUE

I am surrounded by
His blessings on all sides.
I cannot escape.

I feel myself to be
a little drop in the
ocean of His Heart.

The more I draw from it,
the more richly it flows.
I am overrun.

A hidden, infinite
treasure only asking
to show me Itself,

and diffuse, distribute
Its gifts and graces to
enrich my poorness.

19. ST. MARGARET MARY ALACOQUE

Belonging wholly to
the Heart of Jesus Christ,
that is the way to make
sure of our salvation.

When we are completely
consecrated and pledged
to this lovable Heart,

to love and honor It,
abandoning ourselves
entirely to It,

Our Lord takes care of us
and He sees to it that
in spite of all the storms

we come safely into
the port of salvation.

I.iii

THE WALLED GARDEN

SONG OF SOLOMON 8:13

O you who dwell in the gardens,
my companions are listening for your voice;
let me hear it.

PSALM 84:1–5

How lovely is thy dwelling place,
O Lord of hosts!
My soul longs, yea, faints
for the courts of the Lord;
my heart and flesh sing for joy
to the living God.

Even the sparrow finds a home,
and the swallow a nest for herself,
where she may lay her young,
at thy altars, O Lord of hosts,
my King and my God.
Blessed are those who dwell in thy house,
ever singing thy praise!
Blessed are the men whose strength is in thee,
in whose heart are the highways to Zion.

20. JOHANNES TAULER

She was fervent in heart
for her heart was always
opened unto the Lord   *united with*
and it penetrated
the depths of the Godhead.
For she had found there that
which she most dearly loved.   *In her*
By her inner sweetness   *the Heaven*
she was so well-pleasing   *in her*
unto the Almighty;   *the Garden*

by her love, clinging to   *in her*
the Eternal Goodness   *the Palace*
who gave her power   *and she*
over all that He had.   *the Divine*
She lived not to herself   *she needed*
but unto Him alone.   *diator*
All she did was in God
and was full of a pure
and godlike intention.
For she was at all times

the Lord

spirit
of God
soul
of God
body
of God
was filled with
Brightness
no me-
with God.

and never turned away,
not once, from His Presence.
Likeness of no creature
was ever found in her;
with the angels, she saw
all things simply in God;
and she found God alone
at all times in the depths
and being of her soul,
in her spirit. Therefore,

she did not go forth with
all her powers to seek
for the great and varied
but always she abode
in God and God in her.
And with all her powers
she meditated on
the source from which she came.
She was more a creature
of heaven than of earth.

Rapt in the spirit
she came to in a
house of great beauty.
She recognized it
as the Heart of Christ;
she had so often
entered in this way.

Falling to the ground
she discovered there
a large wooden cross
and fell upon it.
A sharp golden dart
sprang from the middle
of the cross, pierced her.

Deep into her soul
she heard the Lord say,
All the wealth on earth
could gladden no soul.
Its health and glory
consist in pain and

in tribulation.

Her soul became sad
and anxious because
she heard the soft voice
of her Beloved
yet could not see Him
standing before her
in a silk garment.

Taking her hand, He
spoke to her softly.
When she felt how soft
this smooth garment was
her soul had begun
to wonder at it.

The Lord answered her,
*Just as silk clothing
is soft to the touch,
every pain and woe
is sweet to a soul
that truly loves God.*

He opens the door to his Heart,
the treasury of the Divine,
and within is a green vineyard.
There is a river of living
water flowing from east to west,
feeding the whole of the vineyard.
Around the river are twelve trees
bearing twelve different kinds of fruit:
charity, peace, joy, and the rest.
This stream, river of charity.

The soul dives into this river,
finding all refreshment in it,
and there she is cleansed of all sins.
In this river is a great school
of fish that have bright golden scales;
they signify all loving souls
who have torn themselves away from
all earthly delights and have plunged
in the fountain of all goodness,
the Sacred Heart of Jesus Christ.

23. ST. MECHTHILD OF HACKEBORN

The virgin Mechthild once prayed
the Lord to grant her this gift,
that the remembrance of Him
would cling to her heart always.

And the Lord showed her His Heart
in the form of a great house.

Flying like a dove, her soul
entered right through its doorway
and found a heap of wheat there.

And the Lord said to Mechthild,
when a dove comes to some wheat
it takes what most pleases her.

When you read or hear the Word
you cannot grasp everything
with your full understanding.

But gather into yourself
a few things with which you can
train your memory and think,

"What is your Lover saying,
what is He commanding you,
in this moment, this lesson?"

The Divine Heart is the
treasury of heaven
from which precious gold has
already been given
to us to pay our debt
and to purchase heaven.
It is the last resource
of His love which He holds
out to us so that
we may profit from it.

And He wishes that in
sanctifying ourselves
we glorify this Heart,
which has suffered more than
the rest of the nature
of our Lord Jesus Christ.
For from the first moment
of the Incarnation,
this Heart was engulfed in
a sea of bitterness.

It suffered from Its first
moment of life until
His last breath on the cross.
Everything His Sacred
Humanity suffered
on the cross His Divine Heart
felt continuously.
That is why God wishes
Christ's Heart to be honored
with special devotion.

In this way, men give Him
as much joy and pleasure
by their love and homage
as they did bitterness
and anguish by the pain
they inflicted on Him.
There is nothing sweeter,
more efficacious than
the ardent charity
of this lovable Heart.

25. ST. FRANCIS DE SALES

Drawn by love, the Beloved comes
into His garden when He comes
into the loving soul; for His
delights are with the sons of men.
Where can He better dwell than where
His Own Image and Likeness is?
It is a verdant garden where
He Himself has planted all the
delight we feel in His Goodness,
wherein we feed, as His Goodness
also feeds on our own delight.

And this reciprocal pleasure
excites that incomparable
love of complacence whereby the
soul is the Beloved's garden
and renders Him its pleasant fruits.
It draws God's Heart to its own heart.
He sheds His precious balms therein.
The King brings me in His chambers.
What are the chambers of the King
but His Breast, full of sweetness
to His Own, through His Sacred Heart.

26. ST. JOHN EUDES

The Divine Heart of Christ
is a port of safety
where the soul is sheltered
from the winds and the storms
of the seas of this world.

In that most Sacred Heart
there is a calm that fears
neither thunder nor storm.
Therein one tastes delight
that knows no bitterness.

There one meets a joy that
knows nothing of sadness.
In it, one possesses
perfect felicity,
quiet serenity.

That same Heart is the first
principle of all good,
the initial source of
all the joys and delights
of paradise.

In a great house there are not only vessels of gold and silver but also of wood and earthenware, and some for noble use, some for ignoble. If anyone purifies himself from what is ignoble, then he will be a vessel for noble use, consecrated and useful to the master of the house, ready for any good work. So shun youthful passions and aim at righteousness, faith, love, and peace, along with those who call upon the Lord from a pure heart.

27. ST. MECHTHILD OF HACKEBORN

A harp proceeds from the Heart of God.
The harp is the Lord Jesus Himself,
but its strings are all of the elect
who have become one in God through love.

Jesus, supreme Cantor of cantors,
strikes the harp, and all the angels sing
Eternal praise to the three Persons,
the Lord has chosen you as His bride!

All the saints chant with sweet harmony,
All now give thanks to God the Father;
He has enriched this Soul with His Grace.
Blessed be the Lord God forever!

28. ST. GERTRUDE THE GREAT

For my beloved Jesus
sings continually sweet
a song of love in my heart
for which I am glorified
by the whole court of heaven.

My ears are entertained with
a ravishing melody
My opened eyes now behold
a most bright glorious light
My nose inhales and mouth tastes
a sweet fragrance and flavor.

II.i
DIVINITY

DEUTERONOMY 6:4–6

Hear, O Israel: The Lord our God is one Lord; and you shall love the Lord your God with all your heart, and with all your soul, and with all your might. And these words which I command you this day shall be upon your heart.

JEREMIAH 32:39–41

I will give them one heart and one way, that they may fear me for ever, for their own good and the good of their children after them. I will make with them an everlasting covenant, that I will not turn away from doing good to them; and I will put the fear of me in their hearts, that they may not turn from me. I will rejoice in doing them good, and I will plant them in this land in faithfulness, with all my heart and all my soul.

2 SAMUEL 7:21–22

Because of thy promise, and according to thy own heart, thou hast wrought all this greatness, to make thy servant know it. Therefore thou art great, O Lord God; for there is none like thee, and there is no God besides thee, according to all that we have heard with our ears.

JOB 10:13

Yet these things you hid in your heart;
I know that this was your purpose.

29. ST. MAXIMILIAN KOLBE

The Holy
come upon you,
power of the
will over

Jesus became the God-Man
to reveal His love for us,
so also, the Third Person,
God-Love, willed to show his me-
diation with the Father
and the Son, and He did so
in an external image,

Mary's Imma

The Holy Spirit lacks fruitfulness in God, meaning that
no Divine Person proceeds
from Him. But He becomes fruitful through Mary whom He has
taken to Himself as Spouse.
With her, in her and through her
the Spirit produces the
Incarnation of the Word.

Spirit will
and the
Most High
shadow you

It should not be thought that the
Blessed Virgin had brought fruitfulness to the Holy Ghost.
As God, He would already
have had this fruitfulness just
as the Father and the Son,
though He had not revealed it,
in that no Divine Person
proceeds from the Holy Ghost.

culate Heart.

Rather, the Holy Ghost has
deemed to manifest his fruitfulness by the media-
tion of Mary, of which he
does not absolutely need,
making the human nature
of Christ through her and with her.

The Sacred Heart of Jesus,
incalculable treasure,
containing the marvelous
riches of heaven and earth
in nature, grace, and glory,
in all the angels and saints,
in the Blessed Virgin Mary,
in the Holy Trinity,
in all Divine perfections.

His Heart is a most precious
treasure house containing all
of the merits of His life,
the fruits of His mysteries,
all the graces merited
by His toils and sufferings.
Everything great, rich, precious,
in Creator and creatures
is stored in that treasure-house.

To whom does this Heart belong?
It belongs to all of us
and to each one in himself.
It depends only on us
to take possession of it.
By what titles and deeds does
this treasure belong to us?
By the title of a gift.
Who has given it to us?

The Father of Jesus has
given it to us, giving
us his Son, and He gives Him
to us continuously,
for His gifts are permanent.

The Son of God has also
given time and time again
in giving Himself to us.
He gives to us ceaselessly
in the Blessed Eucharist.

The Holy Spirit imparts
it to us incessantly,
all of His perfect virtues,
all the gifts of the Spirit
wherewith Christ was so endowed.

31. ST. JOHN EUDES

The Sacred Heart of Jesus,
whether it is considered
in His divinity or
in His humanity, is
more ardently enkindled
with love for His Father,
loving Him infinitely
more at any given time
than all the hearts of angels
and saints together can love
Him through all eternity.

32. ST. JOHN EUDES

Our Savior, as God, has
but one and the same Heart
with the Divine Father
and the Holy Spirit.
His humanly divine
and divinely human
Heart is but one also
with the Heart of the Father
and the Holy Spirit,
by a union of mind,
of love, and of the will.

Therefore, to adore the
Sacred Heart of Jesus
is to adore the Heart
of the Father, of the
Son, and of the Spirit,
to adore a Heart that
is a burning furnace
of love towards us.
Into that hot furnace
we have to plunge so as
to burn there forever.

Unhappy they who are
cast into the furnace
of the eternal fire
that is prepared for the
devil and his angels,
but blessed are they who
shall be thrown into the
eternal fire of love
that enkindles the Heart
of the Father, the Son,
and Holy Spirit.

This commandment which I command you is not too hard for you, neither is it far off. It is not in heaven that you should say, "Who will go up for us to heaven, and bring it to us, that we may hear and do it?" Neither is it beyond the sea, that you should say, "Who will go over the sea for us, and bring it to us, that we may hear and do it?" But the word is very near you; it is in your mouth and in your heart, that you can do it.

33. ST. JOHN EUDES

O love, plunge my mind deep
into that Sacred Heart
as into a river,
burying all of my
negligences and all
of my sins in the flood
of Thy Divine mercies.
In the Heart of Jesus
let me find clarified

all my understanding,
my affections made pure,
and let me have a heart
free, detached and empty
of all imperfections,
so at the hour of death,
when love separates soul and body,
I may return my heart
clean to the hands of God.

All-loving Sacred Heart,
whom I love above all,
you are the one my heart
calls with all affection.
Please be mindful of me,
and may the sweetness of
Thy charity restore
and strengthen the weakness
of my heart.

34. ST. FRANCIS DE SALES

Listen to that Divine Heart
singing its ineffable
song of praise.
He urges us in His Love
Rise up, My love, My fair one,
come away.
Come away to that land where
all is joy, blessing, and praise.

Flowers appear on the earth,
the singing of birds is come,
the turtle
is heard in our land. . . . Arise
My love, My fair one, and come.

Thou may behold Me better
through the clefts of the rock
the pierced side
where My Body was rudely
rent asunder on the cross.

Let Me hear thy voice, beloved,
let it blend wholly with Mine own of
thine own will
so that thy voice shall be sweet
and thy countenance comely.

Never will there be such a
sweetness in our hearts as when
our voices,
united with the Savior's
shall take part in the boundless
praise offered
by the Beloved Son's Heart
to the Eternal Father.

II.ii
SUFFERING

PSALM 69:20–21

Insults have broken my heart,
so that I am in despair.
I looked for pity, but there was none;
and for comforters, but I found none.
They gave me gall for food,
and for my thirst they gave me vinegar to drink.

PSALM 22:14

I am poured out like water,
and my bones are out of joint;
my heart is like wax,
it is melted within my breast.

35. ST. JOHN EUDES

Our Lady united her Heart
to His concerning the Passion,
gave her consent to the painful
death of her dearly Beloved
so that He might abolish sin.

Mary's sacrifice demonstrates
a hatred of sin greater than
suffering the torments of all
imaginable pits of hell,
to take part in its destruction.

If Our Lady had made her choice,
she would have preferred all such pains
rather than see the treatment of
her beloved Son at the time
of His cruel, demeaning Passion.

36. ST. PETER CANISIUS

My soul fell prostrate before your Divine Heart,
my dull deformed soul, ill with the pain of sin,
unclean, infected with vices and passions.
But you, my Savior, opened to me your Heart
in such a way that I seemed to see within
and you invited me and bade me to drink
the waters of salvation from that fountain.

After I had thus dared to approach your Heart,
all full of sweetness, to slake my thirst therein,
you promised a robe to cover my bare soul,
woven out of peace, love, and perseverance.
With this robe of grace and gladness about me
I grew confident that I lacked for nothing
and that all things would turn out to your glory.

37. ST. MARGARET MARY ALACOQUE

The Sacred Heart is
an inexhaustible
fountain of mercy.
It seeks only to
fill humble hearts full,
hearts emptied of self,
bound down to nothing,
so that they may be
ever ready to
sacrifice themselves
to His good pleasure,
no matter how much
it may cost nature.

Since love
one in
if we love,
base our

For one cannot love
without suffering;
He clearly showed us
this upon the cross.
It is still the same
every day in the
Blessed Sacrament.
There He ardently
desires we conform
our whole life to His,
completely effaced
and hidden away
from the eyes of man.

makes lovers
their likeness,
let us
lives on His.

38. ST. MECHTHILD OF HACKEBORN

When you are sick
I embrace you
with my left arm,
when you are well,
with my right arm.

But you should know
when my left arm
embraces you,
My Heart is joined
closely to you.

A thousand fall
at thy left hand
and ten thousand
at thy right hand
yet no evil
shall come nigh thee.

39. ST. MARGARET MARY ALACOQUE

Set up your abode
in this loving Heart
and you will find there
lasting peace and strength
to bring fruition
to all good desires
He inspires in you
to avoid every
deliberate fault.

And place in this Heart
all your sufferings.

Everything that comes
from the Sacred Heart
is sweet. He changes
everything to love.

40. POPE FRANCIS

Passion

The Heart of Christ is not
a pious devotion,
for us to feel some warmth.
It is no tender image
that arouses affection.
It is a passionate Heart,
a Heart wounded with love
and torn open for us.
Pierced, He gives; in His death
He gives us life.
Surmounted by the cross
and surrounded by thorns
it shows us the suffering
our salvation cost our Lord.
That Heart reveals God's passion.
What is it? It is Man, us.

Comfort

Consolation indicates
strength that does not come from us
but from those who are with us.
That is where our strength comes from.
Jesus, who is God-with-us,
gives us strength, His Heart gives us
courage in adversity.
We need this consolation.
The Heart of Christ beats for us,
always saying,
Courage! Do not be afraid.
I am greater than your ills.
He takes you by the hand and
caresses you. He is close,
compassionate and tender,
He is your consolation.

Finally, all of you, have unity of spirit, sympathy, love of the brethren, a tender heart and a humble mind. Do not return evil for evil or reviling for reviling; but on the contrary bless, for to this you have been called, that you may obtain a blessing. . . .

But even if you do suffer for righteousness' sake, you will be blessed. Have no fear of them, nor be troubled, but in your hearts reverence Christ as Lord.

This gentle Virgin
spent all of her life
in such perfect love
to God

that she had never
loved any other
creature that exists
beside God.

No image ever
interposed between
her heart and her love
for God.

Her deep love of God
was undivided,
she loved all creatures
in Him.

She communed within
the depths of her heart,
wherein lay hidden
the Divine Image.

There she
innermost
of her soul,
all powers
and prayed
one

She confessed in her
song of praise that she
could not worthily
praise God;

therefore she desired
that He would praise and
magnify in her
Himself.

From the bottom of
her heart she was so
completely conformed
to God,

that if anyone
had looked there he would
have seen God in all
His Glory,

the procession of
Son and Holy Ghost;
her heart never turned
from God.

dwelt in the
temple
and turned
within
there to the
God.

II.iii
HUMILITY

PSALM 131

O Lord, my heart is not lifted up,
my eyes are not raised too high;
I do not occupy myself with things
too great and too marvelous for me.
But I have calmed and quieted my soul,
like a child quieted at its mother's breast;
like a child that is quieted is my soul.
O Israel, hope in the Lord
from this time forth and for evermore.

MATTHEW 11:28–30

Come to me, all who labor and are heavy laden, and I will
give you rest. Take my yoke upon you, and learn from me;
for I am gentle and lowly in heart, and you will find rest for
your souls. For my yoke is easy, and my burden is light.

The angel Gabriel stood close by her
and found her exalted in spirit.
He greeted her reverently, saying,
Hail, full of grace, the Lord is with thee.
She was troubled by this lofty greeting
because of her deep humility,
and because she was so absorbed in God.

Then, *Behold the handmaid of the Lord,*
and the Holy Ghost took the purest blood
of her Virgin Heart, which had been set
alight by the powerful flame of love,
and created therewith a pure and
perfect little Body, pure, holy Soul,
and so united them together.

This, the Person of the Son of God,
who is the Eternal Word and the
Brightness of the Glory of the Father,
took unto Himself and united it
with Himself in Unity of Persons,
out of love and mercy for our salvation.
Thus, *the Word was made flesh and dwelt among us.*

43. ST. MECHTHILD OF HACKEBORN

Good Jesus, I praise you.
Whatever lacks in me
I ask you to supply.
Good Jesus, I love you.
Whatever lacks in me
offer instead your Heart
to the Father for me.

44. ST. MARGARET MARY ALACOQUE

You must have recourse
to the Sacred Heart
in all of your needs.

Make your abode there
so far as you can.
He will make up for
what is wanting in
your imperfect deeds,

and sanctify your
good ones, if only
you conform yourself
to His holy will.

He will procure much
glory for Himself
through you, if you will
just let Him do so.

45. ST. MARGARET MARY ALACOQUE

If you want to live wholly for Him
and attain what He desires for you,
you must make a complete sacrifice
of yourself and of all that you have,
without reserve, to His Sacred Heart.

You must no longer will anything
but the will of His most loving Heart,
and love nothing except with His love.
Act only according to His lights,
do nothing without asking His help.

Thank Him for the ill as well as the
good success of your undertakings,
never worrying about a thing.
As long as His Heart is satisfied,
loved, and glorified, that is enough.

All the glory must be His alone.

The Savior, when He comes,
shall transform the body
of our humility,
make it like unto the
body of His glory,
provided that our heart
has been transformed, and made
like the humility
of His Heart.

Therefore He said to us:
Learn of Me for I am
meek and lowly of heart.
Remark that there are two
kinds of humility:
one is of conviction,
the other of feeling,
or as it is here called,
of the heart.

By the first we are made
to see our nothingness;
this we can learn ourselves.
And by the second kind,
even in our weakness,
we are thus enabled
to trample under foot
the glory of the world
by His Heart.

We learn this from Him who
emptied Himself and took
the form of a servant,
who, when He was sought for
to be made a king, fled;
and when He was sought for
to endure the shameful
cross, presented to all
His Heart.

Some gain Divine Grace
directly from the
Heart of Jesus Christ,
others from His Hands.

But the further from
His Heart one draws it,
the more difficult
it is to obtain.

Who draws from His Heart
gains more easily,
and much more sweetly
and abundantly.

Those who draw direct
from His Sacred Heart
are those who conform
themselves entirely
to the Divine Will,
who desire above
all things that this Will
should be accomplished
in them entirely.

These ones touch God's Heart
and gain the torrent
of Divine Sweetness,
with much abundance.

But those who have drawn
their help from other
parts of the Body
of our Lord Jesus

are those who labor
to acquire virtue
by their natural
inclinations.

The fear and hardship
they experience
is proportionate
to the extent to
which they have relied
on their own judgment
and so have failed to
submit themselves to
Divine Providence.

Love makes God come down to earth
and raises man to heaven,
unites God and man so close
it makes God man and man God.
Time becomes eternity,
immortal becomes mortal,
mortal is made immortal.

It causes the enemy
of God to become His friend
and His slave to be His son.
Virtue indescribable,
which transforms dirt into God,
changes earth into heaven,
makes me one with my Belov'd!

What shall I render to Thee?
O my soul, why are you not
utterly inflamed, consumed
when you dare to enter by
the Sacred Wound of His side,
into the burning furnace
of His Divine loving Heart?

49. ST. MARGARET MARY ALACOQUE

I hope we may be able
to quit and forget ourselves,
that we may hereafter see
only our One and our All.
That is what He wants of us.
For that reason we must try
our very best to enter
into His sweet loving Heart
by making ourselves quite small,
by humbly acknowledging
our nothingness in which we
must always remain buried.
We must establish a reign
of peace in His Sacred Heart.
This we do by conforming
ourselves to His good pleasure.
To this we must abandon
ourselves as to always take
special care to abolish
all that can be a hindrance.
We must let Him do in us,
with us, and for us His will,
so that He may perfect us
in His own way, and fashion
us according to His will.

But Mary kept all these things, pondering them in her heart.

POPE BENEDICT XVI

Christian piety must involve the senses, which receive their order and unity from the heart, and also the feelings, which have their seat in the heart. It is clear that such piety, centered in the heart, corresponds to the image of the Christian God, who has a heart.

50. ST. MECHTHILD OF HACKEBORN

I give you My eyes,
to see everything with them.
I give you My ears,
to understand all you hear.
I give you My mouth,
to utter all that you should,
speaking, praying, or singing.
I give you My Heart
to consider everything,
in loving Me and all things
for My sake.

With these words God drew the soul
totally into Himself,
uniting Himself with her.

It was then she
saw with God's eyes,
heard with God's ears,
spoke with His mouth.
She had no heart
other than His.

51. ST. GERTRUDE THE GREAT

Taste the sweetness of these holy delights,
be adorned with all virtues, not your own
but those virtues given to you by God

You will hear a most melodious sound,
a sweet harper harping upon His harp.
This music, these words will be sung to you:

Veni mea ad me
Intra meum in me
Mane meus mecum

Come to Me, because I love you
and desire that you should always
be with Me, My beloved spouse

I delight in you, I desire
that you should enter into Me
because I am the God of love

I desire that you should remain
indissolubly united
to Me, even as the body

is united to the spirit
without which the body cannot
live for a moment

HEBREWS 4:12

For the word of God is living
and active, sharper than any two-edged sword, piercing to the divi-

sion of soul and spirit, of joints and marrow, and discerning the thoughts and intentions of the heart.

MATTHEW 10:34–39

Do not think that I have come to bring peace on earth; I have not come to bring peace, but a sword.

EARS OF THE HEART

PSALM 19

Day to day pours forth speech,
and night to night declares knowledge.
There is no speech, nor are there words;
their voice is not heard;
yet their voice goes out through all the earth,
and their words to the end of the world.

ST. PIO

You must speak to Jesus also with the heart, beside the lips; indeed, in certain cases you must speak to him only with the heart.

52. JOHANNES TAULER

Mary was united,
without intervention,
made one Spirit with God
in the depths of her heart

above all created
gifts and graces and lights
in one single light that
renewed unceasingly

thus she had some concept
of future blessedness
and loved God with endless
and uncreated love

all created gifts, works,
virtues, and disciplines
of the earthly creature
must here remain without

she was molded herein
with divine and holy
brightness above all sense
and imagination

she saw eternal lights
as they are in heaven
with unspeakable and
divine joy and pleasure

53. ST. GERTRUDE THE GREAT

He speaks to the heart
of His beloved
and not to her ear.
For His language is
such as cannot be
understood in an
ordinary way.
For these things that are
spoken to the heart
are felt and not heard.

The soul can answer
to the language of
the heart with that
which is most pleasing
to God, to maintain
inner patience and
to desire that the
entire will of God
be accomplished in
her and through her heart.

The answer does not
reach heaven in the
manner of human
communication,
but resounds through that
sweet Divine organ,
the Heart of Jesus,
the ecstatic joy
of the Trinity
and heavenly host.

54. POPE FRANCIS

The pierced Heart of God is eloquent,
It speaks without words.
For it is mercy in its pure state;
love wounded gives life.

How many words we say about God
without showing love!
But love speaks for itself, and it does
not speak of itself.

ST. AUGUSTINE

He was drawn toward a kind of sweetness, an inward, secret pleasure that cannot be described, as though some musical instrument were sounding delightfully from God's house. As he still walked about in the tent he could hear this inner music; he was drawn to its sweet tones, following its melodies and distancing himself from the din of flesh and blood, until he found his way even to the house of God. . . .

In God's home there is an everlasting party. . . . From that eternal, unfading festival melodious and delightful sound reaches the ears of the heart, but only if the world's din does not drown it. The sweet strains of that celebration are wafted into the ears of one who walks in the tent and ponders the wonderful works of God in the redemption of believers . . . (*Exposition on Psalm 42*).

55. ST. JOHN EUDES

Open our ears to the Sacred voice
of the wounds of Thy Body and Heart.
These wounds are so many mouths through which
you call to our hearts unceasingly.

Redite, praevaricatores, ad cor.
Return, you transgressors, to the heart,
which means to My Heart that is all yours,
since I have given it all to you.

Return to the Heart of your Father,
which is so full of love and mercy,
which will receive you and welcome you,
heaping upon you all His blessings.

A trumpet proceeds from God's Heart
to the heart of the soul, then back
from the soul to the Heart of God.

The trumpet's many golden valves
are blest souls that glorify God
in heaven through time unending.

III.i

ALTAR–FIRE

ACTS 13:22

He raised up David to be their king, of whom he testified and said, "I have found in David, the son of Jesse, a man after my heart, who will do all my will."

2 SAMUEL 5:4–5

David was thirty years old when he began to reign, and he reigned forty years. At Hebron he reigned over Judah seven years and six months; and at Jerusalem he reigned over all Israel and Judah thirty-three years.

1 CHRONICLES 21:26; 22:1

And David built there an altar to the Lord and presented burnt offerings and peace offerings, and called upon the Lord, and he answered him with fire from heaven upon the altar of burnt offering. . . . Then David said, "Here shall be the house of the Lord God and here the altar of burnt offering for Israel."

57. ST. JOHN EUDES

Accompanied by Joseph,
she abode with the Savior
for the space of thirty years.

Our Redeemer came on earth
to save man, yet for teaching
He set aside but three years;

to the ever-increasing
sanctification of His
holy Mother, thirty years.

What a wealth of graces and
blessings He incessantly
poured into the soul of His
Blessed Mother.

With flames
enkindling
the virgin heart
worthy

especially when those Hearts
were so close to each other
while she bore Him in her womb,
nursed, and held Him.

For the whole time that she lived
of heavenly fire,   with Him familiarly,
more and more   as a mother with her child,
of His most   firmly bonded,
Mother,

eating and drinking with Him,
praying with Him, and having
the divine words coming from
her Savior's mouth,

so many bright coals of fire,
enkindling more and more
her holy virgin heart with
Love's sacred fire.

58. ST. GREGORY THE GREAT

The fire on the altar
it shall not
the priest
on it
and he shall
the fat of
Fire shall be kept burning
it shall not go out

For the altar of God is our heart
in which the fire is ordered to burn
because it is necessary that
the flame of love
should constantly rise therefrom to God
And we should put on wood ev'ry day
lest it be extinguished forever

Our new life within daily grows old
by its very converse with the world
Fire is fed by a supply of wood
so that while it wastes itself away
by the habits of our condition
it may revive by the examples
of the Fathers
and the testimonies of the Lord

And it is in this rightly ordered
that wood should be thrown on ev'ry day
in the morning
For these things are not done, unless when
the night of blindness is extinguished
Morning is the first part of the day
and everyone of the faithful
must put aside the thoughts of this life
and must enkindle by ev'ry means
the zeal that is failing within him

shall be kept burning on it,
go out,
shall burn wood
every morning,
burn on it
the peace offerings.
upon the altar continually;
—Leviticus: 6:12–13

Whoever kindles this fire of love
within himself, he places himself
upon it as a burnt offering
because he burns out every fault
that wickedly lives within his heart
For when he examines his secrets
and sacrifices his wicked life
he places himself on the altar
of his own heart
kindles himself with the fire of love

And the fat of the peace offerings
it smells sweetly
For the inner fatness of new love
making peace between ourselves and God
emits from us the sweetest odor
And since this selfsame love continues
inextinguishable in the heart
of the Elect, there it is subjoined

And this is that perpetual fire
The fire on this altar will not fail
because the glow of love increases
in their hearts even after this life
Eternal contemplation's effect
Almighty God loved the more deeply
the more He is seen

He made me repose
on His Sacred Breast
where He there disclosed
marvels of His love,
inexplicable
secrets of His Heart,
which up to then He
had concealed from me.

His fire

My Divine Heart is
so inflamed with love
for man and for thee,
being unable
any longer to
contain in itself
the ardent flames of
burning charity.

It must needs spread them
abroad by thy means,
to enrich them with
the precious treasures
that contain graces
and the salvation
to withdraw them from
perdition's abyss.

burns always

I have chosen thee
as an abyss of
unworthiness and
ignorance for the
accomplishment of
this tuneful design,
so that everything
may be done by Me.

60. ST. MECHTHILD OF HACKEBORN

Within His open Heart is
a flame, tall as two palm trees.
Its color is marvelous,
its form indescribable.
I want hearts to burn like this,

in the fire of charity.

When in solitary prayer
let your heart rise up to God.
Such conversation with God
makes the heart catch fire and burn
with the pure love of His Heart.

62. ST. MARGARET MARY ALACOQUE

The Sacred Heart
appeared as a
resplendent sun,   upon
the burning rays
of which fell down

61. ST. MARGARET MARY ALACOQUE

Our hearts must now certainly
be consumed incessantly
in this burning furnace of
the Sacred Heart of Jesus!
Not being able to hold

Its myriad flames

It shoots them forth ardently
into hearts It finds ready
to be inflamed by His love.
How we ought ever to be
inflamed by such burning flames.

my heart,

inflamed with fire
so fervid that
it seemed as if
it would reduce
me to ashes.

Now it was in the heart of David my father to build a house for the name of the Lord, the God of Israel. But the Lord said to David my father, "Whereas it was in your heart to build a house for my name, you did well that it was in your heart; nevertheless you shall not build the house, but your son who shall be born to you shall build the house for my name."

III.ii

THE PASSION

PSALM 40:6–8

Sacrifice and offering thou dost not desire;
but thou hast given me an open ear.
Burnt offering and sin offering
thou hast not required.
Then I said, "Lo, I come;
in the roll of the book it is written of me;
I delight to do thy will, O my God;
thy law is within my heart."

PSALM 22:14

I am poured out like water,
and all my bones are out of joint;
my heart is like wax,
it is melted within my breast.

PSALM 69:19–21

Thou knowest my reproach,
and my shame and my dishonor;
my foes are all known to thee.
Insults have broken my heart,
so that I am in despair.
I looked for pity, but there was none;
and for comforters, but I found none.
They gave me poison for food,
and for my thirst they gave me vinegar to drink.

63. ST. BRIDGET OF SWEDEN

Think on the Passion of my Son
whose members were as my members
whose Divine Heart was as my heart.

He was within me as other
children were in their mother's wombs.

But He was a child conceived from
the charity of Divine Love,
while other children were born from
the concupiscence of the flesh.

When He was born, I felt like half
of my heart was born and went out.

And when He so often suffered,
I felt like half my heart suffered.
Hence, He was to me as my heart.

So my heart was pierced, like my Son's.
I was nigher to Him in His

Passion, and I did not leave Him.
And I stood nearer to His cross.

As what is nearer to the heart
wounds more keenly, my Son's pain was
keener to me than to others.

When He looked at me from the cross
and I at Him, my eyes streamed tears.

When He beheld me spent with grief
all the pain of His own sore wounds
was, as it were, dulled at the sight
of the grief in which He saw me.

Hence, I say boldly, that His pains
were mine because His Heart was mine.

As Adam and Eve sold the world
for an apple, so my Son and
I redeemed the world with one Heart.

When you desire to praise Me
but cannot because of pain,
ask Me to praise and bless God
along with you for that pain.

Let me offer the same praise
I offered to the Father
in my pain upon the cross,
the same gratitude with which
I thanked Him for willing Me
to suffer pain for the world,
and the same love by which I
gladly, willingly suffered.

Just as my Passion bore fruit,
your pains, or any troubles,
if you entrust them to Me,
will bear fruit enough to give
glory to all in heaven,
merit to all the righteous,
pardon to contrite sinners,
relief in purgatory.

For what is so good that my
Divine Heart can't make better?
Every good thing flows from the
goodness of My Sacred Heart.

Undisputed mast'ry
of my heart was His aim
and this, my earthly life
would be one of suff'ring
like His. He would become
my Master, just for this
so that I would become
aware of His presence
and behave like our Lord
in His own cruel suff'rings
which He showed me he had
endured for love of me.

The effect on my soul
was so deep, I wouldn't
have had my suff'rings cease
even for a moment.
He hasn't left me since
and from then on I would
see Him there on the cross
or carrying His cross.
In the pity and love
that filled my tender heart
at seeing such a sight
my own suff'rings seemed light.

Our Lord's sufferings
were great, because of
His soul's suffering.
His soul began to
suffer before His
bodily Passion,
in the agony
in Gethsemane.
*My soul, sorrowful
even unto death.*

The anguish was such
that it burst open
on His whole body,
a violent pang
affecting His Heart;
as in the deluge
the floods of the great
deep were broken up
and the windows of
heaven were opened.

In this living death
He remained, from the
time of agony
while in the garden.
His first agony
was within His soul
and so was His last.
The scourge and the cross
did not begin it
and did not end it.

It was the profound
anguish of His soul
not of His body
that had caused His death.
His persecutors
were thus surprised to
hear that He was dead.
How, then, did He die?
That tormented Heart,
it broke and He died.

That agonized Heart,
which at the start so
awfully relieved
by bursting His pores,
would have broken then
had He not kept
it from breaking.
Soon the time came.
He gave the word
and His Heart broke.

Tormented Heart,
it was love, fear,
grief, that broke Thee.
It was the sight
of human sin,
the feeling of
it laid on Thee.
It was the zeal
for God's glory,
horror at sin

so near to Thee,
a sickening,
stifling feeling,
deep shame, disgust,
and abhorrence
that it inspired,
keen pity for
the souls whom it
has drawn headlong
into hell.

All these feelings
together Thou
didst allow to
rush upon Thee.
Thou didst submit
to their powers.
They were Thy death.
And that strong Heart,
that all-pure Heart,
was slain by sin.

O most tender
and gentle Lord,
when will my heart
have a portion
of Thine own Heart,
when will my hard
and stony heart,
my proud heart, my
unbelieving
and impure heart

be melted and
conformed to Thine?
O please teach me
to contemplate
Thee, that I may
become like Thee
and love Thee most
sincerely and
simply as Thou
hast loved me.

67. ST. GERTRUDE THE GREAT

I reflect devoutly
on the love of Thy Heart
when hanging on the cross
and draw from this fountain
waters of devotion
to wash away my sins.

The unction of mercy
the oil of gratitude
which the sweetness of this
inestimable love
supplies as remedy
for all adversities.

Efficacious charity
as a lasting ligament
of my justification
to unite all my thoughts, words,
and works indissolubly
and powerfully to Thee.

68. ST. JOHN HENRY NEWMAN

Mighty God of love! it is too much!
it broke the Heart of Thy Son Jesus
to see the misery of mankind
spread out full before His very eyes.
He died by it as well as for it.
We, too, in our measure, our eyes ache,
and our hearts sicken, and our heads reel,
when we but feebly contemplate it.

O most sweet, tender Heart of Jesus
why wilt Thou not end, when wilt Thou end
this e'er-growing load of sin and woe?
when wilt Thou chase away the devil
into his own hell, and close the pit,
that Thy chosen may rejoice in Thee,
quitting the thought of those who perish
eternally in their willfulness?

PSALM 16:9–10

Therefore my heart is glad, and my soul rejoices;
my body also dwells secure.
For thou dost not give me up to Sheol,
or let thy godly one see the Pit.

69. ST. JOHN EUDES

Savior, extend the power
of Thy eternal arm to
separate me from myself
and unite me to Thee.
Take my miserable heart
and replace it with Thine own,
enabling me to say:
I will give thanks to the Lord with my whole heart.
I will praise Thee with my heart,
with Your Heart, which is my own.

Sacred Heart of my Savior
be Thou the Heart of my heart,
the soul of my soul,
the spirit of my spirit,
the life of my life,
and the sole principle of
all my thoughts, words, and actions,
the faculties of my soul
and of all my senses,
both interior and exterior.

O what mind can conceive
the tiniest of sparks
of this flaming furnace
of love for the Father?

It is a love that most
perfectly equals the
untold perfections of
its beloved object.

Here is the Son Jesus
infinitely loving
His Eternal Father
who is infinite love.

Here is love in essence
loving eternal love;

a love that is boundless   a love that is boundless
incomprehensible   loving in turn   incomprehensible
infinite   infinite
and passing all limits   and passing all limits.

III.iii

THE PIERCE

LUKE 2:34–35

Simeon blessed them and said to Mary his mother,
"Behold, this child is set for the fall and rising of many in Israel,
and for a sign that is spoken against
(and a sword will pierce through your own soul also),
that thoughts out of many hearts may be revealed."

ZECHARIAH 12:10

And I will pour out on the house of David and the inhabitants
of Jerusalem a spirit of compassion and supplication, so
that, when they look on him whom they have pierced, they
shall mourn for him, as one mourns for an only child, and
weep bitterly over him, as one weeps over a first-born.

ZECHARIAH 13:1

On that day there shall be a fountain opened for the
house of David and the inhabitants of Jerusalem
to cleanse them from sin and uncleanness.

71. ST. BERNARD OF CLAIRVAUX

The love of Christ is a dart
that pierced the soul of Mary
transfixed it from side to side
so it left no part of that

Virgin Heart empty of love
and she loved with all her heart,
all her soul, and all her strength
and was thus hailed, full of grace.

Or perhaps it may be thus
that the dart had transpierced her
in order to penetrate
even to us, so that we

might receive of that fulness
that she might be the mother
of charity, of which God
who is Love, is the Father.

This was done so that she might
bring forth and set firmly her
tabernacle in the sun,
that Scripture might be fulfilled,

which says, *I will give thee for*
a light to the Gentiles, that
thou mayst be My salvation
to the ends of the earth.

This was fulfilled by means of
Mary, who made visible
Him who was invisible
and the Virgin had conceived

not of the flesh nor with the
flesh, because she received through
all her chaste being a wound
one of Love, deep, sweet, and wide.

72. ST. BONAVENTURE

put out your hand
into My side
be not faithless
but believing

be like the dove
that rests in a
hole in the cliff
keeping watch there

like the sparrow
that finds a home
like turtledoves
hide your young there
your chaste love's fruit

come press your lips
to the fountain
draw water from
the Savior's wells

this is the spring
flowing out from
the middle of
the promised land

dividing in-
to four rivers
inundating
all devout hearts

and watering
the whole of earth
rendering it
fertile and rich

run to this source
of life and light
you who are vowed
to God's service

cry out to Him
eager desire
with all the strength
within your heart

untold beauty
of the Most High
pure radiance
life, giving life

light, source of light
eternal light

preserving in
everlasting
splendor the bright
myriad flames

that shone from
the throne of your
Divinity
from dawn of time

and from your Heart
flows the river
that gladdens the
City of God

and makes us to
cry out with joy
and thanksgiving
in hymns of praise

for we know by
experience
that with you is
the source of life

and in your light
we see the light

73. ST. BONAVENTURE

Consecrated souls,
come by love, approach
Christ covered in wounds,
Jesus crowned with thorns.

With the apostle,
do not merely put
finger to the scars,
your hand in His side.

By way of the gate
opened at His side
penetrate all the
way into His Heart.

There, transformed in Him
by your love for the
crucified Divine,
await no other

consolation than
the capacity
to die on the cross
with Jesus Christ.

With the apostle,
shout out, *I have been
crucified with Christ.
It is no longer
I who live but Christ
who lives in me.*

74. ST. FRANCIS DE SALES

My hope is that you will be like
the dove in the cleft of the rock,
in the pierced side of the Savior.

You behold the Savior's pierced side,
and wish to take His Heart and place It
into your own, as if It were
a king in his little kingdom.

Though His Heart is greater than yours,
nevertheless It will contract
so that It can accommodate
Itself to fit the straitened room.

May that Heart live always in ours.
May that Blood flow in our soul's veins.
Let us remain, holy abode.

1. God's love seated within
the Heart of the Savior
as on a royal throne

beholding through the cleft
of the pierce in His side
the heart of ev'ry man

this Heart is King of Hearts
this Heart remains so fixed
on our hearts, without end

2. Who peers through a lattice
sees most clearly the one
who only half sees him

So to the Divine Love
that is the Heart of hearts
sees clearly our own hearts

He gazes upon us
with the eyes of His Heart
we through a glass darkly

3. If we saw His whole Heart
since we are but mortal
we'd die of love for Him

just as when He came down
and took on mortal flesh
died for us out of love

just as He would still do
were His Heart not drawn up
into immortality

76. POPE BENEDICT XVI

1. This Heart is not concerned
with self-preservation
but with self-surrender

by opening Itself
it saves the world
the resulting collapse

of His open Heart
reveals the matter of
the Easter mystery.

2. This Heart calls to our heart
it calls us to step forth
from our futile attempt

to preserve our own lives
and join in the task
of His Divine Heart's love

to discover the love
that is eternity
and which sustains the world.

3. O God! if we could hear
this Divine Heart singing
voice infinitely sweet

His canticle of praise
to the Divinity
O what joy, what striving

our hearts would so desire
to spring up to heaven
to hear it forever.

O Lord, behold my heart
detached from all creatures
offered to Thee freely.

Do Thou purify it
in the sanctifying
waters of Thy pierced side.

Don it with the precious
Blood of Thy sweetest Heart
and unite it to Thee
by charity's odors.

78. ST. GERTRUDE THE GREAT

O most loving Lord,
by Thy piercèd Heart
pierce my heart with the

arrow of Thy love
so nothing earthly
may remain therein

and that it may be
so completely filled
with the power of
Thy Divinity.

Then he brought me back to the door of the temple; and behold, water was issuing from below the threshold of the temple toward the east (for the temple faced east); and the water was flowing down from below the south end of the threshold of the temple, south of the altar. Then he brought me out by way of the north gate, and led me round on the outside to the outer gate, that faces toward the east; and the water was coming out on the south side. Going on eastward with a line in his hand, the man measured a thousand cubits, and then led me through the water; and it was ankle-deep. Again he measured a thousand, and led me through the water; and it was knee-deep. Again he measured a thousand, and led me through the water; and it was up to the loins. Again he measured a thousand, and it was a river that I could not pass through, for the water had risen; it was deep enough to swim in, a river that could not be passed through. And he said to me, "Son of man, have you seen this?"

Then he led me back along the bank of the river. As I went back, I saw upon the bank of the river very many trees on the one side and on the other. And he said to me, "This water flows toward the eastern region and goes down into the Arabah; and when it enters the stagnant waters of the sea, the water will become fresh. And wherever the river goes every living creature which swarms will live, and there will be very many fish; for this water goes there, that the waters of the sea may become fresh; so everything will live where the river goes. Fishermen will stand beside the sea; from En-ge'di to En-eg'laim it will be a place for the spreading of nets; its fish will be of very many kinds, like the fish of the Great Sea. But its swamps and marshes will not become fresh; they are to be left for salt. And on the banks, on both sides of the river, there will grow all kinds of trees for food. Their leaves will not wither nor their fruit fail, but they will bear fresh fruit every month, because the water for them flows from the sanctuary. Their fruit will be for food, and their leaves for healing."

CLOSING

PSALM 45:1

My heart overflows with a goodly theme;
I address my verses to the king;
my tongue is like the pen of a ready scribe.

2 CORINTHIANS 3:2–3

You yourselves are our letter of recommendation, written
on your hearts, to be known and read by all men; and
you show that you are a letter from Christ delivered by us,
written not with ink but with the Spirit of the living God,
not on tablets of stone but on tablets of human hearts.

79. ST. JOHN EUDES

Mary considered and honored
the Divine Will as her last end,
the center of her existence,
knowing that she existed in
the world only to accomplish
the Creator's will in all things.
All her thoughts, words, and actions were
directed only to this end.
In this amiable center
her pure Heart exclusively sought
and found its contentment and rest.

80. JOHANNES TAULER

what more could he do
that he has not done?

he opened his Heart
a secret chamber
to place my own heart
his desired spouse

his joy is to be
in silent stillness
to rest with me there
in peaceful silence

he gave me his Heart
within which to live
until I am cleansed
and without blemish

until I am made
like unto his Heart
made fit and worthy
to be led with him

into the Divine
Heart of the Father

he gives me his Heart
that it be my home
he desires my heart
that he might dwell there

he gives me his Heart
as a resting place
purple with his blood
set with red roses

in return
he asks for my heart
set with white lilies
of good works

God's plan and ruse are not yet perfected;
means to enter the world's interior,
in order to transform it from within,
with which to break open the bolted gate.

Then it was that God created a Heart
and placed it at the center of the world.
It was a human Heart, and It knew all
impulses and yearnings of human hearts,
and was experienced in all windings,
wanderings, changes of weather, and drives.
So It was fully experienced in
the bitter joy and joyful bitterness
any human heart has ever savored.

The human heart is of all God's creatures
most foolish, most obstinate, most fickle.
Seat of fidelity and treachery,
instrument richer than an orchestra,
yet poorer than a lone grasshopper's chirp.
In its incomprehensibility
a wan and obscured mirror image of
God's own incomprehensibility.

This is the thing He drew from the world's rib
as it slept, and He fashioned it into
the very organ of His Divine Love;
with this weapon He knew all from within.

Thou didst burst and break through agony
in the garden of Gethsemane
and Thy precious contents trickled out
through the veins and pores of the skin
upon the earth. And again, Thou hast
been drained all but dry upon the cross.
After death, Thou wast pierced by the lance
and gavest out the small remains
of that inestimable treasure,
our redemption.

Sacred Heart, Thou beatest for us still.
Thou dost condescend to suffer me
to receive Thee, to eat and drink Thee.
O make my heart beat with Thy Heart.
Purify it of all earthly things
that neither the events of the day
nor the circumstances of the time
may have power to ruffle it
but that in Thy love and in Thy fear
it may have peace.

Is it possible Thy Sacred Heart is
suspended, a lamp in the midst of mine,
which is so unworthy of its presence

when at the same time I have the pure joy
of finding in you this very same source
of all that is worthy and delightful?

*It is even so. When you wish to take
hold of anything, you stretch forth your hand
and withdraw after you have taken it.*

*So also the love that I bear for you
makes Me send my Heart to draw you to Me
when you distract yourself with worldly things.*

*And when you have recollected yourself
I withdraw My Heart and your heart with it
so that you may enter into Me.*

Thus you taste the sweetness of all virtues.

84. ST. BONAVENTURE

How wonderfully deep
is Mary's humility.
An archangel salutes her;
she is then called full of grace;
she is told the Holy Ghost
will come and overshadow her;
she becomes the Mother of God;
she is raised above all creatures;
she is appointed sovereign
Lady of both heaven and earth;
and yet instead of becoming
filled with pride, she humbles herself:
Behold the handmaid of the Lord.

Behold, you desire truth in the inward being;
therefore teach me wisdom in my secret heart.

To me, though I am the very least of all the saints, this grace
was given, to preach to the Gentiles the unsearchable riches
of Christ, and to make all men see what is the plan of the
mystery hidden for ages in God who created all things.

APPENDIX I: ABOUT THIS BOOK

This book is not simply a collection of meditations on the Sacred Heart. There is also a hidden aspect which may require explanation for those who have noticed that there is an unusual arrangement to these and want to know more.

We recognize the book, the particular arrangement of paper, glue, and other materials, as a simple medium for words and whatever else may go along with them: pictures, tables, and the like. A book may be well-designed and beautiful, but this does not necessarily have to do with the meaning in the text. Modern production methods necessitate this bias towards the text, and suggest that the text contains all of the meaning, and the book is only a conveyor of that meaning or in some cases a helpful assistant to it. eBooks are a good example; readers can adjust the text font and layout to their liking.

While it may appear that this book is like any other in this sense, it is not made in this way. The design and layout are symbolic, and in a way today's reader may not recognize. If this book were to be published in a new edition, with a different design and layout, it would lose its meaning as a compilation and the symbolism that it is built upon.

In the Middle Ages, books were made out of the skins of animals. This was not lost on some who recognized a correspondence between the "flesh" without and the "meaning" within. This implies a sacramental view of reality, where material reality — including books — participates in the spiritual reality of God. The Incarnation is the ultimate example of this. St. Bonaventure called Christ "the book written within [the Word] and without [the flesh] for the restoration of the world." The Sacred Heart exemplifies this reality, as a symbol both of the life-sustaining organ of Christ's body and the "heart" of who He is, the God-man. It is not inappropriate then to conceive of a book on the Sacred Heart as a symbol of this deep truth, one that points to a mystery, wherein we can be hidden within the Sacred Heart.

Some medieval authors designed their manuscripts such that the words shaped the "flesh" of the parchment; the words determined the form of the book, just like the Word was embodied in physical reality.

This old (and largely forgotten) way of making books could be seen as having a theological parallel with the Sacred Heart devotion. The Sacred Heart is a heart of flesh: "And the Word became flesh and dwelt among us." Analogously, the versified saints' "words" are united with the "flesh" of the book. The authors' voices are "embodied" in the book, and so the book contains the means to discover the voice hidden within it. The text cannot be understood fully without experiencing its grounding in the material.

Isaiah says: "Truly, Thou art a hidden God, the God of Israel, the Savior!" For us, Paul adds: "For you have died, and your life is hidden with Christ in God." The believer is hidden with Christ in the hidden God! But God has not spoken in secret. When the Word became flesh, God came into His creation. If we have seen the Son, we have seen the Father. This profound mystery can also be made a symbol in books, where the text is apparent to us but the deeper meaning calls to us. Any book about the Sacred Heart is insufficient to describe it, but in faith and prayer the text is surmounted, and we have an experience with the Heart Itself.

This also suggests one simple reality about books that is sometimes not recognized. When we read well, we piece together the elements—the words, paragraphs, pictures, and so on—into a whole and coherent narrative. But this is not done effectively if we have not trained ourselves to read well. We do not necessarily do all of this work consciously, but the means by which we do it is fundamental to our understanding. The design and layout of this book is meant to aid this effort by incorporating the medieval notion of sacramentality into the act of reading. The symphony that can be discovered in the words of the saints points us to the loving and harmonious work of the Holy Spirit. If we meditate on these texts, written over the course of centuries, we can approach the Oneness of God who inspired such words.

I have briefly explained some elements of this mode of reading, but not the design element of the book. That would defeat the purpose, that it is meant to be discovered. For us today, who have developed different reading habits from the Middle Ages, it is a puzzle, a mystery to be worked out by experience and close attention. It is the same with the Sacred Heart. It is a mystery we can enter into to discover the depths of God's love.

APPENDIX II: SOURCES

Alacoque, St. Margaret Mary. *The Autobiography of St. Margaret Mary Alacoque*. TAN Books, 2012.
> Poems: 59 (p. 53); 62 (p. 55).

Alacoque, St. Margaret Mary. *The Letters of St. Margaret Mary Alacoque: The Apostle of the Sacred Heart*. Translated by Fr. Clarence A Herbst, S.J. TAN Books, 2012.
> Poems: 3 (pp. 222–23); 5 (p. 172); 11 (pp. 229–30); 18 (pp. 124–25); 19 (pp. 43–44); 24 (pp. 221–22); 37 (p. 75); 39 (p. 74); 44 (p. 38); 45 (p. 37–38); 49 (pp. 134–35); 61 (p. 225).

Augustine, St. *Earlier Writings*. Selected and translated with introductions by John H. S. Burleigh. The Westminster Press, 1953.
> St. Augustine quote on p. vi (p. 258).

Augustine, St. *Expositions of the Psalms, 33–50*. Vol. III/16. Translation and notes by Maria Boulding, ed. John E. Rotelle. New City Press, 2000.
> St. Augustine quote on p. 43v (p. 247).

Balthasar, Hans Urs von. *Heart of the World*. Translated by Erasmo S. Leiva. Ignatius Press, 1979.
> Poems: 6 (pp. 47–48); 81 (pp. 44–45).

Bernard of Clairvaux, St. *Life and Works of Saint Bernard, Abbot of Clairvaux*. Vols. III and IV. Edited by Dom. John Mabillon, translated by Samuel J. Eales. London, 1896.
> Vol. III—Poems: 1 (p. 342); 14 (p. 315); 46 (pp. 275–76).
> Vol. IV—Poem: 71 (p. 191).

Bernard of Clairvaux, St. *On the Song of Songs I*. Translated by Kilian Walsh. Cistercian Publications, 1981.
> Poem: 4 (pp. 152–54).

Bernardine of Siena, St. "From sermon 9 on the Visitation." Our Lady of the Rosary Old Roman Catholic Church. Accessed May 26, 2025. https://www.rosarychurch.net/mary/imheart.html.
> Poem: 7.

Bridget, St. *Revelations of St. Bridget, on the Life and Passion of Our Lord, and the Life of His Blessed Mother*. Translated by William H. Neligan. New York, 1862.
> Poem: 63 (pp. 79–80).

Eudes, St. John. *The Admirable Heart of Mary*. Translated by Charles di Targiani and Ruth Hauser. P.J. Kenedy & Sons, 1948.
> Poems: 15 (p. 58); 35 (p. 145); 79 (p. 236); 84 (p. 232).

Eudes, St. John. *The Sacred Heart of Jesus*. Translated by Dom Richard Flower, O.S.B. P.J. Kenedy & Sons, 1944.
> Poems: 9 (p. 62); 16 (p. 63); 26 (p. 77); 30 (pp. 46–47); 31 (p. 2); 32 (p. 40); 33 (pp. 75–76); 48 (p. 61); 55 (p. 38–39); 57 (p. 7–8); 69 (pp. 100–1); 70 (p. 1).

Falque, Emmanuel. *God, the Flesh, and the Other: From Irenaeus to Duns Scotus*. Translated by William Christian Hackett. Northwestern University Press, 2015.
> Poem: 73 (p. 193).

Francis, Pope. *Homily of His Holiness Pope Francis*. Catholic University of the Sacred Heart, November 5, 2021.
> Poems: 40, 54.

Francis de Sales, St. *Of the Love of God*. Translated by H. L. Sidney Lear. London, 1888.
> Poems: 2 (p. 60); 25 (pp. 150–51); 34 (p. 171).

Francis de Sales, St. *The Saint Francis de Sales Collection*. Catholic Way Publishing, 2015.
> Poem: 74 (pp. 2132–33).

Francis de Sales, St. *Treatise on the Love of God*. Vol. 1. TAN Books, 1975.
> Poem: 75 (p. 263).

Gertrude, St. *The Life and Revelations of Saint Gertrude, Virgin and Abbess, of the Order of St. Benedict*. London: Burns & Oates, 1866.
> Poems: 13 (p. 187); 28 (pp. 50–51); 47 (pp. 189–90); 51 (pp. 185–86); 53 (pp. 35–36); 67 (p. 83); 77 (p. 190); 78 (p. 82); 83 (p. 184).

Gregory the Great, St. *Morals of the Book of Job*. Vol. III. Oxford, 1847.
> Poem: 58 (pp. 104–6).

Kerns, Vincent, ed. and trans. *The Autobiography of St. Margaret Mary*. Darton, Longman & Todd, 1976.
> Poem: 65 (p. 7).

Kolbe, St. Maximilian. "Why Mary is Our Mediatrix." Servants of the Pierced Hearts of Jesus and Mary. Accessed April 7, 2025. https://www.piercedhearts.org/hearts_jesus_mary/heart_mary/mary_mediatrix_kolbe.htm.
> Poem: 29.

Mechthild of Hackeborn, St. *The Book of Special Grace.* Translated by Barbara Newman. New York, Paulist Press, 2017.

 Poems: 8 (p. 156); 10 (p. 195); 17 (pp. 169–70); 21 (pp. 170–71); 22 (p. 157); 23 (pp. 200–1); 27 (p. 156); 38 (p. 176); 43 (p. 213); 50 (p. 177); 56 (p. 159); 60 (p. 191); 64 (pp. 180–81).

Newman, St. John Henry Cardinal. *Discourses Addressed to Mixed Congregations.* Longmans, Green, and Co., 1902.

 Poem: 68 (pp. 41–42)

Newman, St. John Henry Cardinal. *Meditations and Devotions of the Late Cardinal Newman.* Edited by Rev. W. P. Neville. Longmans, Green, and Co., 1907.

 Poem: 66 (pp. 323–25); 82 (pp. 412–13).

O'Donnell, Timothy Terrance. *Heart of the Redeemer: An Apologia for the Contemporary and Perennial Value of the Devotion to the Sacred Heart of Jesus.* 2nd Edition. Ignatius Press, 2018.

 Poems: 72 (p. 64); 80 (p. 68); 36 (p. 72).
 Pope Benedict quote on p. 40 (p. 32).

Pio of Pietrelcina, St. "Counsels from the Heart." Servants of the Pierced Hearts of Jesus and Mary. Accessed April 7, 2025. https://www.pierced-hearts.org/theology_heart/counsels_of_%20heart/counsels_st_pio.htm.

 St. Pio quote on p. 41.

Prayer of St. Bonaventure.

 Poem: 12

Ratzinger, Joseph Cardinal. *Behold the Pierced One: An Approach to a Spiritual Christology.* Translated by Graham Harrison. Ignatius Press, 1986.

 Poem: 76 (p. 69).

Tauler, John. *The Inner Way, being Thirty-Six Sermons for Festivals by John Tauler, Friar-Preacher of Strasburg.* Translated by Arthur Wollaston Hutton. Edwin S. Gorham, 1900.

 Poems: 20 (pp. 76–77); 41 (p. 59); 42 (pp. 78–79); 52 (pp. 63–64).